12-17

Sikhism

Major World Religions

Buddhism

Christianity

Hinduism

Islam

Judaism

Sikhism

MAJOR WORLD RELIGIONS

Sikhism

Jennifer Burton

MASON CREST
PHILADELPHIA

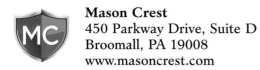

Mason Crest
450 Parkway Drive, Suite D
Broomall, PA 19008
www.masoncrest.com

Printed and bound in the United States of America.

CPSIA Compliance Information: Batch #MWR2017.
For further information, contact Mason Crest at 1-866-MCP-Book.

First printing
1 3 5 7 9 8 6 4 2

Library of Congress Cataloging-in-Publication Data

on file at the Library of Congress
ISBN: 978-1-4222-3821-9 (hc)
ISBN: 978-1-4222-7974-8 (ebook)

Major World Religions series ISBN: 978-1-4222-3815-8

QR CODES AND LINKS TO THIRD-PARTY CONTENT

Table of Contents

KEY ICONS TO LOOK FOR:

Words to understand: These words with their easy-to-understand definitions will increase the reader's understanding of the text while building vocabulary skills.

Sidebars: This boxed material within the main text allows readers to build knowledge, gain insights, explore possibilities, and broaden their perspectives by weaving together additional information to provide realistic and holistic perspectives.

Educational Videos: Readers can view videos by scanning our QR codes, providing them with additional educational content to supplement the text. Examples include news coverage, moments in history, speeches, iconic sports moments and much more!

Text-dependent questions: These questions send the reader back to the text for more careful attention to the evidence presented there.

Research projects: Readers are pointed toward areas of further inquiry connected to each chapter. Suggestions are provided for projects that encourage deeper research and analysis.

Series glossary of key terms: This back-of-the book glossary contains terminology used throughout this series. Words found here increase the reader's ability to read and comprehend higher-level books and articles in this field.

A ceremonial guard patrols near the Golden Temple of Amritsar, in the Punjab region of India. Sikhs consider this complex to be the holiest place of worship (gurdwara) in Sikhism.

 # Words to Understand in This Chapter

amrit sanskar—the ceremony at which Sikhs become members of the Khalsa.

gurdwara—literally, "doorway to the Guru"; the Sikh place of worship, anywhere that the Guru Granth Sahib is installed, whether a purpose-built building or one converted from another use, a room in a home or a tent in a field.

gurmukhi—literally, "from the mouth of the Guru"; the special script in which the Guru Granth Sahib is written.

Guru Granth Sahib—the Sikhs' sacred scripture, which they believe represents God's living presence among His people.

haumai—a combination of the Punjabi for "I" or "me," often translated as "ego."

hukam—God's will or divine order; the belief that all things happen according to God's will.

jot—God's light, which is present in all living beings and inanimate objects.

kirpan—a sword; one of the Five Ks.

kirtan—literally, "songs praising God"; passages from the Guru Granth Sahib and other approved writers that are set to ragas. One of the most important ways that Sikhs meditate on God's name.

maya—the delusion of attachment to earthly things, rather than to God.

Mul Mantra—literally, "root" or "seed." This mantra is a summary of Sikh teaching about God, the first verse of the Guru Granth Sahib and of the Japji Sahib, a prayer recited by Sikhs each morning.

1 What Is Sikhism?

The word "Sikh" comes from the Punjabi word *shishya*, which means "disciple" or 'follower." Sikhs follow the teachings revealed by God to ten men who are known as the Gurus. These men lived between the years of 1469 and 1708 CE in a region known as the Punjab, on the Indian subcontinent.

"Guru" is a combination of two Punjabi words, *gu* (meaning "darkness") and *ru* ("light"). A guru is someone whom people believe can take away spiritual darkness and bring spiritual light. In India and elsewhere, the word *guru* is often translated as "teacher."

The teachings of the ten Sikh gurus can be summarized by the phrase "one God and one humanity." In the culture of the Indian subcontinent, people were divided into social

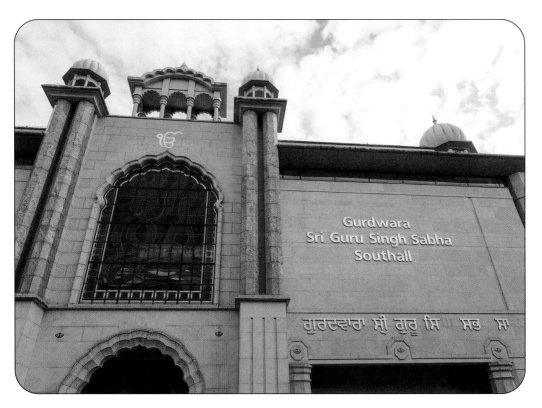

The exterior of a Sikh temple in the Southall neighborhood of London. The United Kingdom has a significant Sikh population because of its former imperial relationship with India and the Punjab region where Sikhism originated.

groups called castes. The caste system determined how important someone was believed to be and the kind of employment that that person could have. Brahmins, the highest caste, were the priests and political leaders. Sudras were the servants. Women were not considered to be members of any caste, nor were they allowed to receive religious teaching, or read sacred scriptures. When a husband died, his wife was expected to commit suicide on his funeral pyre.

The Sikh gurus wanted to eliminate the caste system and change the culture. They taught that all people were equal and that everyone, regardless of their gender or the circumstances of their birth, should be permitted to study religious teachings and take part in worship services.

Sikhs Beliefs About God

Sikh teaching about God is summarized in the *Mul Mantra*—the first words of *Guru Granth Sahib*, the Sikh sacred scripture. These are also the first words of the Japji

Sikhs bow before the Guru Granth Sahib as an act of respect for the sacred scriptures. They regard the Guru Granth Sahib as the living presence of God among His people.

The Mul Mantra

The Mul Mantra is a statement of belief that was written by the first guru, Nanak, the founder of Sikhism. It is the first text of the Guru Granth Sahib, the holy scriptures of Sikhism, and it is repeated more than 100 other times in the scriptures.

The Mul Mantra is the most widely known part of Sikh scripture. It is written in the *Gurmukhi* alphabet, a special script created just for Sihk scriptures for the Punjabi language. Because of this, it is challenging to translate accurately. One translation that comes close to the ideas of the original is as follows: "One God, the Creator of the Universe, Beyond Fear, Beyond Hatred, Beyond Death, Beyond Birth, Self-Existent, by the Guru's Grace."

Sahib, one of the prayers that Sikhs say each morning.

Sikhs believe in one God, who created the world and is present in everything. Not only do all living beings—from people to animals to insects and flowers—have God's *jot* in them, but so too do inanimate objects. Sikhs believe in treating all people equally and in caring for the environment.

Sikhs believe that all living beings and other objects have a beginning, an existence, and an end. When this physical existence finishes, Sikhs believe, God's *jot* within the being returns to earth in the form of another physical existence. This is called reincarnation, and is part of a con-

Sikhism is a monotheistic religion that stresses the importance of doing good rather than merely carrying out rituals. Sikhs believe that the way to lead a good life includes: keeping God in heart and mind at all times; living honestly and working hard; treating everyone equally; and serving others.

Educational Video

To hear the Mul Mantra being chanted, scan here:

stant cycle of birth, life, death, and rebirth.

Only those living things born as human beings can ever be liberated from the cycle. Then, the spiritual light that is in them returns permanently to God. Human beings can achieve this by obeying God's teachings in their daily lives. They can continually meditate on God's name, be honest in their daily lives, and give some of their earnings to help those in need, and serve God and other people.

The Guru Granth Sahib warns Sikhs that they are living in an evil world and should not be corrupted by its many temptations. A Sikh should be like the lotus flower that only grows in stagnant, dirty water but whose flowers sit on the surface of the water and are white and clean. Sikhs are especially warned against two temptations—*haumai* and *maya*. *Haumai* is a combination of words for "I" and "me," and is often described as "ego." It is concerned with what "I" want, and not with obeying God's *hukam*, or will. *Maya* is the delusion of thinking that things such as money and possessions, which are temporary, are important, rather than obeying God, who is eternal.

A Young Sikh's Life Today

Harmeet Kaur is a young Sikh who aspires to follow the

teachings of her faith both in her deeds and in her outward appearance. She lives at home in London with her parents, grandmother, older brother, and younger sister. In the following paragraphs, she describes how she practices her faith in her daily life:

"I come from a religious family. Sikhism has always been the way of life I wanted to follow. When I was 14, I committed myself to it fully and started to attend group discussions about Sikhism led by older teenagers.

Harmeet Kaur lives in London with her family.

"When I was 16, I began to wear a turban, and to follow the daily practice of a committed Sikh. When I was about 18, I made a formal commitment to obey the Sikh way of life at the ceremony called *amrit sanskar*.

"Every morning, I get up at about five o'clock, shower, and then recite the Sikhs' five morning prayers. At seven in the morning, I visit the *gurdwara* with my parents. This is where Sikhs meditate on God's name. We spend about half an hour there in prayer.

"From nine in the morning till five in the afternoon, I attend university. As I work, I try to repeat God's name in my mind, over and over. That does not mean that I am not concentrating. Rather, it is like a child playing with a kite. The child is aware of the kite and makes all the necessary adjustments to keep it in the air, but can still talk to friends at the same time. Repeating God's name in this way should be automatic, but I admit that I have not yet reached that stage.

"For just over a year, I have been learning to play the *sarangi*, a traditional Indian stringed instrument. This is so that I can accompany the *kirtan*—songs praising God—which are an important part of a gurdwara service.

"Once a month on a Saturday evening, young Sikhs play *kirtan* at a local gurdwara. I am not yet a skilled enough *sarangi* player to join in with the musicians, but I do take part in the singing.

"Sometimes the young people from my gurdwara organize a get-together at a Sikh camp. There, we can learn more about our religion from other Sikhs and enjoy activities such as trampolining, holding water fights, and paint-balling.

"I am very keen on sport in general. I play basketball and go running every week. I also like swimming. At all times, I wear a a short sword called a *kirpan*—which is a symbol of my faith—under my clothes, and I carry this wherever I go. It is so important to me that I wear it when I go swimming, in the shower, and when I sleep."

 Text-Dependent Questions

1. What is the Mul Mantra?
2. Who were the ten Sikh gurus? How can their teaching be summarized?
3. What do Sikhs believe happens to people after they die?

 Research Project

The CIA World Factbook website (https://www.cia.gov/library/publications/the-world-factbook) has population and religious adherence figures for all nations. Print out a large map of the world, and note the number of Sikhs living in each country. What countries have the largest number of Sikhs? Why? Do research in your school library or the Internet to support your conclusions.

Sikh devotees in the Punjab region march during a traditional annual festival known as Hola Mohalla.

 ## Words to Understand in This Chapter

gurbani—literally, "God's word"; the words divinely given to the human gurus, which today are recorded in the Guru Granth Sahib.

Khalsa—a community of women and men who, because of their spirituality, have the courage to defend their Sikh faith and the human rights of others.

langar—the communal meal that is available to everyone at a gurdwara.

lavan—literally, "circling"; the four verses of the marriage hymn that are sung at a Sikh wedding while the bridegroom leads the bride in circling the Guru Granth Sahib.

masand—local officials appointed by the guru to give religious teaching, to collect offerings of money given to the guru, and to supervise local *sangats*.

nam japna—the continual meditation on God's name, one of the responsibilities of all Sikhs.

nishan sahib—the triangular flag flown outside a gurdwara. It is usually saffron in color, although it may be dark blue. The Khanda, the symbol of the Khalsa, is shown on it.

panj piare—literally, "beloved ones"; the five Sikhs who offered their heads to the Guru at the festival of Vaisakhi in 1699.

raga—a traditional Indian musical mode, or tune, aimed at putting people in the right emotion to hear and understand the words said.

A Sikh man prays outside of a temple in India. Sikhs believe that repeating a special word or phrase, called a mantra, helps a person to concentrate and not be distracted by personal problems or things going on nearby. This enables the person to relax and achieve spiritual understanding.

2 The History of Sikhism

Sikhism as a formal religion can trace its origins back to the fifteenth century. It began with Guru Nanak, who came from the town of Talwandi, not far from the city of Lahore, in what is today Pakistan.

The region known as the Indian subcontinent, or South Asia, includes three major countries today: India, Pakistan, and Bangladesh. This region has a long history of human civilization, beginning with the Indus River Valley civilizations more than 5,000 years ago. Around the year 1500 bce, invading tribes from Europe and Persia, known as Aryans, intermingled with the Indus River Valley civilizations. This mixture of natives and Aryans gave birth to classical Indian culture and the Hindu religion. Today, most people living in the Indian subcontinent follow Hinduism.

In the 10th and 11th centuries CE, invading Turks and Afghans brought the Islamic faith to India. Islam soon became popular among some Indians.

Around the time of Nanak's birth, South Asia was the scene of a struggle for power. Invading armies led by such figures as Genghis Khan and Tamerlane had tried to conquer India during the thirteenth and fourteenth centuries. In the 1520s, a Muslim warlord named Babur gained control of Lahore and most of the Indian subcontinent. He established the Mughal Empire, which ruled India for hundreds of years.

The Mughal rulers were Muslims, but they had to practice religious tolerance because most people living in the empire were Hindus. However, some rulers were less tolerant than others, so tensions and violence between Hindus and Muslims within the empire were not uncommon.

The Experience of Guru Nanak

Guru Nanak was born in 1469. His family were Hindus, who lived in a region known as Punjab, meaning "land of the five rivers." The Punjab region had been home to some of the Indus River Valley's earliest civilizations. It was a prosperous region that rulers often sought to control. (Today, the part of the historical Punjab region where Nanak was born lies in eastern Pakistan, while the balance is located in northern India.)

There are many stories and legends told about Guru Nanak that indicate that, even from a young age, he was destined to become a person of religious importance.

The Tolerant Mughal Emperor

The Mughal Empire, one of the greatest in Central Asian history, dominated the Indian subcontinent from the 16th to the 18th century. The empire was established by Babur after he overthrew the previous rulers, the Delhi Sultanate, in 1526. While the Mughal rulers were famous for their conquests, they also became known for their promotion of the arts and the beautiful buildings they constructed.

The Sikh religion was able to flourish during the rule of Akbar, one of the greatest Mughal rulers. He reigned over the empire from 1556 to 1605. Akbar extended the Mughal empire and improved the way it was governed. The level of religious freedom that Akbar permitted was unprecedented for a Muslim government. He married both Muslim and Hindu wives, and also explored the beliefs of many different religions, including Christianity and Sikhism.

In an empire in which a minority group of Muslims ruled a Hindu majority, religious tolerance was particularly important. Unfortunately, some of the Mughal rulers who came after Akbar, including his immediate successor Jahangir, were far less tolerant of other religions. This created a greater division between Muslims and non-Muslims in India than ever before, and resulted in the Sikh communities of the Punjab arming themselves to resist persecution.

According to one story, during his first day at school as a young child Nanak said that the only learning that mattered to him was about God. As a young man, Nanak developed a reputation as a person who understood spiritual matters. When he was still a teenager, and working as a

Statue depicting Guru Nanak, the first human Guru, who Sikhs believe was taken into God's presence and given his life's work.

shopkeeper, people would come every evening to hear him teach about God. Nanak would also provide a meal to all those whom he taught.

One morning, while he was bathing in a river, Nanak disappeared. He was 30 years old at the time. Villagers found his clothes on the bank of the river, and believed he had drowned. However, after three days Nanak returned and told the villagers that he had been taken into God's presence. Nanak said that God had told him to spend the rest of his life practicing *nam japna* (meditation on God's name) and teaching others to do the same. Nanak said that God was neither Hindu nor Muslim, and that people needed to focus on God and work toward equality and justice for all people on earth.

After this experience, Nanak traveled around India and beyond, carrying out God's instructions. He became known as *guru*, meaning "teacher." Stories and legends say that he traveled widely, visiting Tibet and the Arabian Peninsula among other places. A musician named Mardana, who was a Muslim, accompanied him.

Guru Nanak told those who heard him preach that God was telling him what to say. He would suddenly feel that God wished him to utter certain words. These words became known as *gurbani*, which is a blending of the Sanskrit words *guru*, meaning "teacher," and *bani*, mean-

Indian women prepare food in the kitchen of a Sikh temple. The practice of eating a communal meal, or langar, was started by Guru Nanak and refined by the gurus who followed him. Today, some Sikh temples serve thousands of free meals each day.

ing "word." To help people remember the *gurbani*, Mardana composed *ragas*—traditional Indian tunes—to fit the words. Guru Nanak's followers used to meet together to sing the *gurbani* and listen to Guru Nanak's teaching. These were the origins of the Sikh religion.

Before Guru Nanak died in 1539, he appointed one of his followers as his successor, naming him Guru Angad. Ultimately, there would be nine gurus who followed Guru Nanak, making ten altogether. Sikh's believe that God's *jot* ("light") was in each of them, and their teachings were one and the same.

If all of the gurus's teachings were the same, why was there a need for ten gurus, one after another? Sikhs believe that everything that happens is according to God's will: there were ten gurus because that is what God wanted. Another explanation is that God's teachings had to be revealed over many years so that people would be able to understand them properly. In a short time, only a limited amount of information can be understood.

The Nine Gurus Who Followed Guru Nanak

The successor to Guru Nanak, Guru Angad, continued the work started by Nanak. Guru Angad refined the practice of the *langar*, or communal meal—an idea that Guru Nanak had initiated. When Sikhs share a meal in this way, they are demonstrating their belief in the equality of all people. Guru Angad also devised a new type of alphabet, known as the *gurmukhi* script, which was used for sacred Sikh writ-

This inscription from a Sikh temple is written in the gurmukhi script, which was developed by the second guru to be used for sacred Sikh writings.

The Taj Mahal, a famous landmark of the Mughal era in India, was built during the reign of Emperor Jahan, son of Jahangir. Jahan's rule from 1628 to 1658 was a relatively peaceful period for the Sikhs of the Punjab.

ings. Like Nanak, Guru Angad traveled widely, spreading the message of Sikhism and establishing new centers of worship. Before his death in 1552, at the age of forty-eight, he passed on all the sacred Sikh writings to his appointed successor, Guru Amar Das.

Guru Amar Das was a contemporary of the first two gurus. He was seventy-three when he took the position. One of his major accomplishments was organizing the Punjab into 22 districts, each with its own *masand*, or local Sikh leader. The masand would be responsible for spreading Sikh beliefs and collecting offerings of money from the faithful on behalf of the guru. Guru Amar Das also started a practice of the guru meeting with the Sikh community during the Hindu festivals of Vaisakhi and Divali.

In 1574, Guru Ram Das became the fourth guru. He founded a town in northern India, now called Amritsar, and added the *lavan*, the Sikh marriage hymn, to the collection of sacred texts known as *gurbani*.

When Guru Ram Das died in 1581, his youngest son succeeded him, taking the name Guru Arjan. He was only eighteen years old when he became the fifth guru. Guru Arjan collected all the *gurbani* that God had given to the first four gurus, and added the writings of some Hindu and Muslim holy men to show that God could be found in all religions. His collection is called the *Adi Granth*. He also supervised the building of the Harmandir Sahib, or Golden Temple, at Amritsar. In 1604, when the building was complete, Guru Arjan installed the *Adi Granth* inside, and bowed before the sacred scripture to show that God's words

Sacred Scripture of the Sikhs

The Guru Granth Sahib comprises the Adi Granth, which Guru Arjan placed in the Harmandir Sahib, and the gurbani given to Guru Tegh Bahadur by God. Shortly before Guru Gobind Singh died, he said that the Guru Granth Sahib would be the eleventh and last Guru and would be called by that name. In future, he said, if Sikhs wanted to know God's will, they should read this sacred scripture rather than ask a human Guru, as they had done before.

were more important than he was. The following year, the Mughal emperor Jahangir began to persecute Sikhs and other non-Muslims. Emperor Jahangir had Guru Arjan arrested, and ordered him to convert to Islam. When the guru refused, he was killed as a martyr in 1606.

Guru Hargobind, who lived between 1595 and 1644, was the son of Guru Arjan. He was only eleven years old when he became the sixth guru. Guru Hargobind wore two swords, to symbolize the idea that as guru he had authority over both worldly and spiritual matters. He ordered the Sikhs to resist persecution by the Muslim rulers of the Mughal Empire, and under his leadership Sikhs were trained in military skills. Emperor Jahangir arrested Guru Hargobind around the year 1611, but soon agreed to release him from prison. The occasion of his release is celebrated by Sikhs at the Divali festival. They hold fireworks displays, send greetings cards, and traditionally give sweets as presents. After this, Emperor Jahangir did stop persecuting the Sikhs for the most part. Jahangir's son and successor, Emperor Jahan, also allowed the Sikhs their freedom to worship after he gained the Mughal throne in 1628.

In 1658, however, Jahan became sick and his son Aurangzeb seized power as the Mughal emperor. He soon did away with the previous policies of accommodation, which had permitted Hindus and Sikhs to live peacefully with the Muslim rulers. During a period of increasing perse-cution, the grandson and successor to Guru Hargobind, named Guru Har Rai, continued to spread Sikh teachings. Although he maintained a Sikh army, Guru Har Rai attempted to avoid fighting and bloodshed with the Mughals. He died of natural causes at age thirty-one in 1661.

Guru Har Krishan was only five years old when he suc-ceeded his father and became the eighth guru. He was

A Place for All

The Harmandir Sahib (Golden Temple) was designed to demon-strate some important Sikh teachings. A Muslim, Mian Mir, laid the foundation stone, showing respect for all religions. The building has entrances on all four sides, indicating that everyone is welcome. The steps leading down are a reminder that everyone should be hum-ble before God. On the ground floor, the Guru Granth Sahib is installed. Upstairs, there is a balcony where people may sit undis-turbed, listening to the kirtan which is played throughout the day.

Harmandir Sahib, in Amritsar, became known as the Golden Temple because of the gold plating that the Sikh Maharajah Ranjit Singh installed when Amritsar became part of his empire in 1802.

known for being kindhearted. During a visit to Delhi, Guru Har Krishan cared for people suffering from a smallpox epidemic. He became infected with the disease himself and died at the age of eight.

The ninth guru, Tegh Bahadur, was a distant relative of Har Krishnan, and was known for his many contributions to the Guru Granth Sahib. He also defended the rights of Sikhs from Muslim oppression. In 1675, Hindus from the Kashmir region asked Tegh Bahadur to protect them from forced conversion to Islam by the ruler of that region, who was a Muslim. Tegh Bahadur traveled to Delhi to meet with the Mughal Emperor Aurangzeb, hoping to resolve the situation but knowing that his life was in danger. When he arrived, the emperor ordered Tegh Bahadur to renounce Sikhism and become a Muslim himself. When Tegh Bahadur refused, Aurangzeb had him publicly beheaded in Delhi in 1675.

The son of Guru Tegh Bahadur, Gobind Singh, was chosen as the tenth guru in 1676. He introduced some new practices, such as the "Five Ks," the articles of faith by which Sikhs were expected to live. Guru Gobind Singh also added new writings to the Guru Granth Sahib, and edited the sacred texts to create the standardized version of the scriptures that Sikhs still use today. At his death in 1708, Gobind Singh told his followers that there would be no other human gurus—going forward, Sikhs would have the Guru Granth Sahib to guide their lives.

Warfare Against the Mughals

Guru Gobind Singh had outlived the Mughal Emperor Aurangzeb, who had died in 1707. Although Aurangzeb had succeeded in conquering new territories for the empire, the Mughal state was collapsing from within. The constant warfare was costly, and the emperor had alienated Sikhs and Hindus with his efforts to convert his subjects to Islam. Although the the Mughal Empire would endure in some form for another 150 years after Aurangzeb's death, it would never regain its past glory. Rebellions by local rulers and wars with foreign powers steadily diminished the

Formation of the Khalsa

In 1699, when Sikhs gathered before Guru Gobind Singh at the festival of Vaisakhi, he stood there, sword in hand, asking who would "offer their head to the guru." One by one, five Sikhs stepped forward to offer their heads, and one by one they were led into a tent. After the fifth volunteer was taken into the tent, they all emerged from the tent, alive and unharmed.

Guru Gobind Singh said these volunteers would be known as the *panj piare*, "the five beloved ones," because they were prepared to give their lives to the guru. They became the first members of the *Khalsa*, a community of women and men who, because of their inner spirituality, have the courage to defend their Sikh faith and the human rights of others. Guru Gobind Singh also introduced the Five Ks—the five items worn by Sikhs to symbolize important Sikh teachings—and a daily code of conduct. In addition, he started the *amrit sanskar*, a ceremony of commitment in which Sikhs become members of the Khalsa.

Today, to commemorate the events of 1699, *gurdwaras* are specially decorated for Vaisakhi and the *nishan sahib*—the flag that flies from the *gurdwara*—is changed. Sikhs make an effort to attend the services, which will include talks about *Guru Gobind Singh* and the commitment of the *panj piare*.

Traditionally, *amrit sanskar* ceremonies are held, and often there is a procession that conducts the Guru Granth Sahib through the streets.

Mughal realm and led to the creation of many small independent states in northern India.

A man named Banda Singh Bahadur, who had converted to Sikhism after hearing Guru Gobind Singh speak, led a Sikh attempt to gain control of the Punjab from Mughal forces after the guru's death. In 1709 his army captured the city of Samana, which the Mughals had used as the capital of Punjab. He soon gained control over the entire region, and set up a Sikh government, while continuing to fight Mughal forces. In 1716 Banda Singh Bahadur was captured by the Mughals and tortured to death.

Educational Video

Scan here for a short video about Sikh warriors:

From 1716 until the 1730s, rulers of the Mughal Empire attempted to eradicate the Sikhs. Many of the Sikhs retreated to a mountain range called the Sivalik Hills, where they waged a guerilla war against against the Mughals. The Sikh army was known as the Dal Khalsa, as it was made up of Sikhs who had been baptized and consecrated as Guru Gobind Singh had commanded.

During the rest of the eighteenth century, Sikhs gradually gained control over some parts of the Punjab. They established a dozen small kingdoms, known as *misls* ("confederacies") in the region. However, although the leaders of the *misls* were Sikhs, the confederacies sometimes fought

Sikhs waged guerilla war against the Mughal Empire from bases and camps in the Sivalik Hills, in the foothills of the Himalayan range.

against each other for power. When non-Sikhs invaded, however, such as Muslims from Afghanistan or from the Mughal Empire, the *misls* worked together to defend the Punjab.

In 1799 an army commanded by Maharaja Ranjit Singh conquered Lahore, which had been controlled by Muslims. Maharajah Ranjit Singh soon united the *misls* and established the Sikh Empire, which would rule the Punjab until 1849.

The town of Pul Kanjari was built by the legendary Sikh leader Ranjit Singh in the early nineteenth century. It is located near the present-day border of India and Pakistan.

The British Arrive in India

The British Raj, or rule over India, had its roots in a commercial enterprise. On December 31, 1600, the British East India Company, a private corporation, was chartered in London. The English government granted the East India Company monopoly rights on all British trade with India and the Far East. Before the end of the 17th century, the East India Company had firmly established itself on the Subcontinent, acquiring trading rights in Madras (1639), Bombay (1664), and Calcutta (1696).

In many respects India proved an ideal place for the British merchants to do business. Europe craved goods from the East, including silk, china, calico, and tea, and labor in India was cheap—one pence a day versus six back in Britain—so the goods were inexpensive to produce.

England wasn't the only European country involved in the Far East trade, however. Over the years, Portugal, France, the Netherlands, and Denmark had competed for the lucrative trade—and the latter three had also chartered private East India companies. By the mid-1700s, the French Compagnie des Indes Orientales, established in 1664, had emerged as a major rival of the British East India Company. In 1744, when European politics drew their respective nations into war, the two companies—which maintained private armies—began fighting each other in India.

European military superiority enabled Great Britain to extend its influence in India. This typically did not involve the direct conquest of local populations, however. Rather, the East India company strategically backed one local ruler against another—in exchange for commercial concessions. (There were many opportunities, as India at the time was breaking apart into hundreds of smaller kingdoms.) By the 1850s, the British East India Company was the richest and most powerful force in the region.

British soldiers fight against Indian troops during their conquest of the subcontinent. The period of British domination of India began in the early seventeenth century, with the British government officially taking control between 1858 and 1947.

Gurdwara Dera Sahib is a Sikh temple in Lahore, Pakistan.

In 1757, a British East India Company army commanded by Robert Clive defeated the Muslim ruler of Bengal, the most populous province of India, at the Battle of Plassey. Clive had allied himself with Sikh and Hindu forces to gain the victory, adding Bengal to the areas under British control. The British East India Company, which previously had been involved only in export trade, soon controlled Bengal's internal trade markets, and by 1764 the Mughal emperor had granted all right to tax collection in that region to the British East India Company.

The British East India Company now controlled a large part of the Subcontinent. Company officials had not planned to conquer India; they were simply businessmen who had taken the most expedient route to profitability—for the company as a whole and, increasingly, for themselves as individuals. Whether through bribery, duplicity, or sheer ruthlessness, they removed all who stood in the way of their accumulation of wealth.

India was very important to England because it generated a huge volume of trade and commerce, and the British East India Company paid the British government a large amount of money every year to maintain its monopoly rights. But the British government eventually became concerned about the administration of India. Some officials in the British government were deeply troubled by the East India Company's methods and believed, with justification, that the organization was rife with corruption and operated largely above British law. Through legislative actions in the 1770s and 1780s, the British government gradually took a greater role in the governance of India.

The dual structure of British authority in India—with trade falling under the purview of the East India Company and the British government taking more responsibility for governance—lasted into the middle of the 19th century. During this period, the armies of the East India Company expanded British control on the Subcontinent. By 1818 the Hindu Maratha states of central India had been conquered. In 1843 the British defeated the Muslim amirs of the Sind. And after two bloody wars, in 1845–1846 and 1848–1849, the East India Company annexed the wealthy Sikh kingdom of Punjab.

Sikhs Leave the Punjab

From the time of Guru Nanak, Sikhs had always been willing to live outside their traditional homeland. The British involvement in India led to a greater migration of Sikh communities and ideas beyond the Punjab and into other lands controlled by the British Empire. Some Sikhs were recruited into the British army during the nineteenth and twentieth centuries. These Sikhs served as soldiers in many parts of Asia, Africa, Europe, or the Americas. After serving in the army, some returned to the Punjab. Others remained in places like Singapore or Hong Kong, where the British had established colonies and Sikh communities flourished. Over the years, other Sikhs moved to places like Indonesia or the Philippines, as well as to Australia, the Fiji Islands, and Canada.

At the end of the nineteenth century, about 32,000 Indian craftsmen, most of whom were Sikhs, left India to build a railway in Uganda. A little more than a fifth of them stayed in Kenya, Tanzania, and Uganda until the 1960s, when many left because of political upheavals in East Africa. They then moved mainly to Britain or Canada.

Canada's first Indian immigrants were Sikhs, who arrived in 1904 to the cities of Victoria and Vancouver, located in the western province of British Columbia. They were attracted to the area after hearing tales from returning British Indian soldiers about the region's beauty and high wages. During the early 20th century, more Sikhs settled in British Columbia than anywhere else in Canada or the United States.

Due to the Sikhs' long and rich military history, it was natural for the British rulers to recruit Sikhs into the British Army. They were generally formed into all-Sikh regiments, and sent to defend British possessions around the globe. (Top) Sikh military officers are featured on a British postcard from 1917. (Bottom) Members of a British Sikh regiment prepare an artillery gun for firing in Singapore, circa 1940.

Sikh immigrants to the United States were processed at the Angel Island station in San Francisco Bay, California, between 1910 and 1940.

The Sikhs worked in logging camps and lumber mills. At that time all Canadians were legally British subjects, and as British citizens, Sikhs had the right to vote. According to Harold Coward, history professor at the University of Victoria, by 1908 about 5,000 Indians had arrived, most of them Sikhs. By that point the area's small white population had felt threatened by the Sikhs' numbers, and anti-immigration sentiment had grown considerably.

In 1908, British Columbia's legislature denied Asian immigrants voting and other rights. The same year Canada implemented the "continuous journey" law, which required South Asians to book passage on a ship traveling without stop from their country of origin. Because no ship line traveled continuously from India to Canada, legal immigration was impossible.

In defiance of the regulation, wealthy Sikh merchant Gurdt Singh Sarhali chartered a Japanese steamer, the Komagata Maru, and brought many Indian immigrants along for a journey departing from Hong Kong. When the ship arrived in Vancouver Harbor on May 23, 1914, with 376 Indians onboard, it received a hostile reception. Its passengers remained isolated for two months, while Canadian authorities refused to allow food and water to be brought aboard. Eventually, the passengers were deported, except for those few who had previously established residency in British Columbia.

Essentially cut off from their families, some of Canada's Indians returned to India or moved to the United States. In the 1920s, a few wives and children of those who remained in British Columbia were allowed to join them. The continuous journey regulation remained in effect until 1947, when it was removed along with the voting and other restrictions.

Britain's first gurdwara opened in 1911 in Putney, a neighborhood in southwest London. This gurdwara later moved to Shepherd's Bush in west London.

Later Waves of Sikh Immigrants

After the Second World War ended in 1945, Britain had a shortage of workers because many men had died in the fighting. Local government authorities and some large companies sent representatives to both the West Indies and the

Sikhs on motorcycles take part in a Canada Day parade in Abbotsford, British Columbia.

Indian subcontinent to encourage men to come and work in Britain. Many of those that answered the appeal were Sikhs.

In the words of one writer, these workers "helped first bandage up Britain's wounds of war and then set it on the road to recovery." Some of the Sikhs who made the move went to Scotland or the English Midlands, but many settled in west London. Today, the west London community numbers about 100,000 Sikhs and is the largest outside India.

The Sikhs who went to Britain before and soon after the Second World War found very few other gurdwaras. Many Sikhs often worked as many as 60 hours a week, and were too exhausted to travel a long way to a gurdwara afterwards. Sometimes they would meet in a nearby house or hire a local hall on a Sunday to practise *nam simran*, or meditation on God's name. As more Sikhs arrived in Britain, and wives and families went over from India, they opened their own local gurdwaras. Usually, these were converted houses or shops, but now there are also purpose-built gurdwaras.

The Singh Sabha gurdwara in west London, was founded by Sikhs who arrived in the 1950s. At first, they hired a local hall for kirtan on Sunday afternoons. Then, in 1961, a gurdwara was opened in a house, moving to a nearby hall as attenders increased. In 1967, the gurdwara moved to Havelock Road, converting a disused factory. It was extended in 1975. In 1999, the old gurdwara was demolished, and a new one, standing seven stories high, was built to replace it. Today it is the largest gurdwara in London, and one of the largest outside of the Punjab region.

 Text-Dependent Questions

1. Who was the first guru? When did he live?
2. What is a *langar*?

 Research Project

Using the Internet or your school library, research the life of one of the ten Sikh gurus. Write a two-page report about this person and present it to your class.

 ## Words to Understand in This Chapter

dastar—a turban worn by men, and some women, to cover uncut hair.

diwan—literally, "court"; the hall in the gurdwara where the Guru Granth Sahib is installed.

granthi—any woman or man who reads the Guru Granth Sahib.

hukamnama—God's word or command, addressed to those present at a *gurdwara* service.

kachhehra—knee-length baggy shorts, also called kachs; one of the Five Ks.

kangha—a small comb worn in the hair; one of the Five Ks.

kara—an iron or steel bangle worn around the wrist; one of the Five Ks.

khanda—a short, double-edged sword; also the name of the symbol of the Khalsa, which is a circle with a two-edged sword in the center and two crossed kirpan, one on either side.

kurahit—lterally, "prohibition"; four actions that are forbidden for Khalsa Sikhs, which include cutting body hair; using tobacco, alcohol, or other drugs; committing adultery; eating halal meat.

Rahit Maryada—the Sikh code of conduct published by the Shiromani Gurdwara Parbandhak Committee on February 3, 1945, and followed by most Sikhs.

sangat—literally, "being together" or "congregation." A gathering of Sikhs to practice *nam japna* or worship together at a local gurdwara.

seva—literally, "service"; this can be service to God by, for example, reading the Guru Granth Sahib, performing *kirtan*, or helping with the *langar* by giving, cooking, and serving the food or cleaning the gurdwara. It can also refer to service done for Sikhs or non-Sikhs outside the gurdwara.

Sikh pilgrims wait in a long line to enter the most important Sikh gurdwara, Harmandir Sahib, in Amritsar, India.

3 Daily Observance of the Sikh Faith

From the time of Guru Nanak, Sikhs have been told that they should continually meditate on God's name; work honestly and give a proportion of what they earn to those in need; and serve God as well as other people. In 1699, at the festival of Vaisakhi, the tenth guru, Gobind Singh, introduced a daily code of conduct called a *rahit* for members of the Khalsa. Since then, there have been various versions of the Sikh codes of conduct. The current version, called the *Rahit Maryada*, was approved by the Shiromani Gurdwara Parbandhak Committee, an elected body of Sikh leaders, in February 1945. There have been minor changes to the code in the decades since then, but no major overhaul has been undertaken.

The first part of the Rahit Maryada states that a Sikh is anyone who believes in:

- one God;
- the ten human Gurus and their teachings;
- the Guru Granth Sahib; and
- the importance of *amrit sanskar*, a formal ceremony of commitment to the Sikh faith.

The Rahit Maryada also states that a Sikh may not belong to any other religion.

A Sikh should rise before dawn, says the Rahit Maryada and, after taking a bath, should recite the morning prayers. Before beginning a new task, a Sikh should pray to God for his blessing. Sikhs also have set prayers to say in the evening and before going to bed. The Rahit Maryada also emphasizes the importance of visiting the gurdwara, participating in the *sangat*, and listening to and meditating on the teachings of the Guru Granth Sahib.

Educational Video

Scan here for a short video on the kirpan.

During the day, everything a Sikh thinks and does should be according to the sacred scripture's teachings. Sikhs are expected to learn the gurmukhi script so that they can read and understand the Guru Granth Sahib. Parents are expected to teach their children about Sikh beliefs and practices.

There are four *kurahit*—prohibitied activities that Sikhs must never do. Sikhs are not permitted to cut any of their bodily hair. They may not use tobacco, alcohol, or other drugs. They are forbidden from commiting adultery, or having a sexual relationship with a person who is not their spouse. And they are not allowed to eat meat from animals that were killed according to an Islamic ritual known as *halal*. Although eating meat that is not *halal* is permitted, many Sikhs are vegetarian.

The Five Ks

There are five things that Sikhs wear to symbolize their faith. All of them begin with "k" in the Punjabi language, so they are known as the "Five Ks." They include:

- *kesh* (uncut hair)
- *kangha* (a wooden comb)
- *kara* or carry (an iron or steel bangle worn on the wrist)
- *kirpan* (sword)
- *kachhehra* or kachs (knee-length baggy shorts)

The Five Ks symbolize important Sikh teachings. For example, to maintain *kesh* symbolizes obedience to God's will. Sikhs believe that hair is natural and given by God, so to cut your hair or shave your beard is breaking God's will. Guru Nanak said that Sikhs should die with their hair intact—"the hair with which they were born." To keep their hair

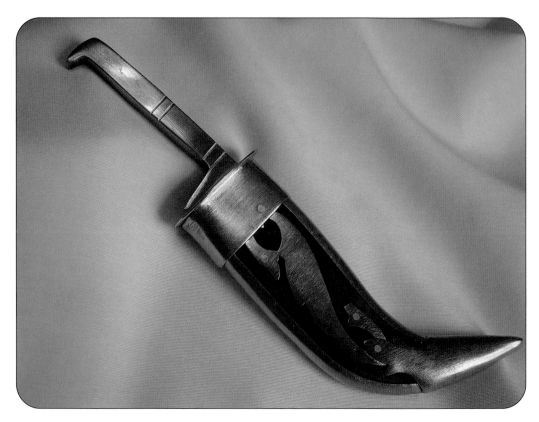

The kirpan is a sword or long knife that Sikhs are required to wear. Sikh teachings say that the kirpan can only be used in self-defense, or to protect others.

covered, Sikh men, and some women, wear a turban. Other women wear a long scarf called a *chunni*. All Sikhs are required to cover their head in the gurdwara.

The *kara*, an iron or steel bangle worn around the wrist is a circle—which, like God, has no beginning or end. A circle is strong, so the *kara* is also a symbol of the strength and unity of the Khalsa.

The *kangha* is the small comb used to comb the hair and to secure the *kesh* in place. It is a symbol that Sikhs should be neat, and tidy, and well-disciplined. The knee-length baggy shorts worn by Sikhs, called *kachhehra* or *kachhs*, symbolize the high moral standard of behavior that Sikhs must practice.

The *kirpan* symbolizes a Sikh's duty to uphold justice and defend those treated unjustly. It can be more than three feet in length, though most *kirpans* worn as part of daily life are between about 6 and 8 inches long. The word *kirpan* comes from two Punjabi words, *kirpa* ("blessing") and *ana* ("honor").

In recent years, questions have been raised about the legality of Sikhs wearing *kirpans* in public places. For most

Sikhs are instructed to keep a kangha comb in their hair. They use it twice a day to clean the hair and remove tangles. Combing their hair reminds Sikhs that their lives should be tidy and organized.

A group of Sikh men in India wear traditional turbans, called dastar. *The* dastar *is an important part of the Sikh culture, and is required for Sikhs who have made a formal commitment to the faith through the* amrit sanskar *ceremony. The turban is worn to cover the Sikh's long, uncut hair (*kesh*).*

people, carrying a sword or an eight-inch-long knife is prohibited by law, but Western governments have approved exceptions because this is a key requirement of the Sikh faith. For example, in Great Britain the Criminal Justice Act of 1988 generally made it illegal to carry a bladed or pointed instrument, but Section 139 of the Act provided for certain exceptions, including for religious reasons. Therefore, a Sikh may lawfully carry a *kirpan* in the United Kingdom.

The laws are similar in Canada and the United States. In both countries, school-age Sikhs are permitted to wear a *kirpan* into school, with the requirement that it be glued or secured into a scabbard so that the weapon cannot be drawn.

Daily Worship at the Gurdwara

There are no special holy days in Sikhism. Some Sikhs try to visit the gurdwara to pray every day. In the United Kingdom, many Sikhs will make a special effort to go to the gurdwara on a Sunday.

Gurdwaras normally open each day at about four in the morning and close at about ten at night. The gurdwara can be visited at any time during these hours. Some Sikhs stay

Inside the Gurdwara

Gurdwara comes from two Punjabi words: *guru* and *duara*, which means "doorway." A gurdwara is any place where the Guru Granth Sahib is kept. The presence of the book is the main reason why Sikhs visit the gurdwara. When they first pass through the doorway and enter the *diwan* ("hall"), they bow down before the Guru Granth Sahib, touching the floor with their forehead, and offer a gift, usually a small coin. In so doing, they show respect for the book. They then sit on the floor, taking care not to point their feet at the book, as this is a sign of disrespect.

Interior of the Gurdwara Bangla Sahib, an important Sikh temple in India. It's known for its association with the eighth Sikh Guru, Guru Har Krishan.

for only for a few minutes, others for several hours. Guru Amar Das said that Sikhs should rise at *amrit vela* ("before dawn"), as this is an especially spiritual time of the day.

The daily services begin when the Guru Granth Sahib is carried down from a special room, where it has been taken to rest for the previous night. Some gurdwaras have a *granthi*—someone employed full time who reads aloud the Guru Granth Sahib to the *sangat*, or congregation. But any Sikh, male or female, who can read the gurmukhi script, in which the Guru Granth Sahib is written, may read the sacred scripture.

After morning prayers, the granthi opens the Guru Granth Sahib at random and reads out the passage at the top of the left-hand page. This is called the *hukamnama*, and is God's message to the *sangat* for the day.

The first *hukamnama* of the day is usually written out and displayed so that people who arrive later can read it. After the *hukamnama*, those assembled stand up and, facing the Guru Granth Sahib, recite the prayer Ardas, during which requests to God may be made. Everyone then cups their hands to receive *karah parshad*, which is made from semolina, butter, and milk. Eating *karah parshad* symbolizes the Sikh belief in the equality of all people. This is fol-

Reading Scripture at Home

Special arrangements have to be made if the Guru Granth Sahib is taken from the gurdwara into the home. The room where the scripture is to be kept must be cleaned, all furniture taken out, and a *takht* (throne) and *chianni* (canopy) put in the room. The family whose home it is will also prepare food, as visitors who come for the Akhand Path reading will be given *karah parshad*, which is made from semolina, butter, and milk. The host family is also expected to prepare a *langar*, or communal meal. The end of the reading will be attended by as many family members and friends as possible.

lowed by kirtan, which lasts for at least an hour and often much longer. There is also a *katha*, a sermon that is either based on a teaching from the Guru Granth Sahib or on an event or story from Sikh history.

Commitment to the Faith

Sikhs formally commit themselves to their faith through the ceremony of *amrit sanskar*, after which they become members of the Khalsa. Before "taking *amrit*," as it is often called, a Sikh must wear the Five Ks and obey the Gurus' teachings in their daily lives. There is no minimum age for undergoing the ceremony, but the person should be old enough to understand the commitments that he or she is making.

Apart from those taking *amrit*, the only people present at the ceremony will be five Sikhs who symbolize the *panj piare*—the original five members of the Khalsa, a reader of the Guru Granth Sahib, and someone to make sure that the ceremony is not disturbed.

Amrit sanskar begins with the opening of the Guru Granth Sahib. One of the *panj piare* explains the Sikh teachings and the promises that the initiates will be making. A prayer is said, and the amrit prepared in a bowl made of iron or steel. As sugar crystals (*pastasas*) are stirred into the water, using a *khanda*, the *panj piare* recite God's words. The recitation takes about two hours. Then, one by one, the initiates come forward, kneel, and are given amrit to drink in their cupped hands. Amrit is then sprinkled five times on their hair and on their eyelids.

The initiates drink any amrit that may be left, then each of them recites five times the Mul Mantra, the opening words of the Guru Granth Sahib. One of the *panj piare* then explains to the initiates the daily code of conduct that they must follow, the Rahit Marayada.

Guru Gobind Singh said that anyone who becomes a member of the Khalsa is a *sant-sipahi*—a person who obeys God's teachings and has the courage to challenge injustice.

Sikhs take *amrit* as an outward expression of their inner spirituality and commitment to God. But all Sikhs, whether or not they have taken *amrit*, are expected to obey God's teachings in their daily lives.

Voluntary Service

Guru Nanak taught that Sikhs should both serve God and help everyone else, whatever their religion or country of origin. This is the concept of *seva*—"service" or "voluntary help."

To Sikhs, serving God by, for example, reading the Guru Granth Sahib in the *gurdwara*, and helping other people are both equally important. The *nishan sahib* flag that flies from a *gurdwara* signifies that any person, Sikh or other, will be given accommodation for a night and a meal free of charge.

Every gurdwara offers *langar*, a communal meal that is served whenever the gurdwara is open. Traditionally, people eat this meal sitting cross-legged on the floor, but usually a few tables are available for the elderly and those with young children. Some people, and not just Sikhs, visit the

Sikh men hold up signs during the annual Sikh Day parade and festival in New York City. The sign on the right refers to incidents of violence against Sikhs that have occurred in the United States since the September 11, 2001, terrorist attacks. Some people have attacked Sikhs, believing them to be Muslims because of the dastar *that observant Sikhs wear.*

gurdwara every day for their main meal. The langar provides opportunities for people of all ages to perform *seva* by, for example, cooking or serving the food, or afterward cleaning the pots and pans. Because of this, the Rahit Maryada describes the *langar* as the "laboratory of *seva*."

Gurdwaras help both Sikhs and non-Sikhs in other ways too. For example, a gurdwara in Hounslow, west London, organizes a sponsored walk every year, to pay for eye clinics in India. It has also encouraged its members to register as bone marrow donors to help sick people in Britain. Gurdwaras also arrange to help people with financial or legal problems, as well as those who are unemployed and looking for jobs.

Seva can be done anywhere and can include many different kinds of service. In Great Britain, Canada, and the United States, there are Boy Scout troops for Sikh communities, to meet the needs of young people. Although the leaders of the troops are all Sikhs, boys and girls of any religion are welcome to join.

To celebrate the 300th anniversary of the Khalsa, a group of young people in west London founded Khalsa Aid in 1999. This is a humanitarian relief organization that helps people across the world, regardless of their religion or ethnic background. In recent years Khalsa Aid has provided financial assistance to help with the Syrian refugee crisis, victims of 2016's Hurricane Matthew in Haiti, and many other worthwhile causes.

 Text-Dependent Questions

1. What does a *granthi* do?
2. What is the *hukamnama*? How is it chosen?
3. What is the purpose of the *amrit sanskar* ceremony?

 Research Project

Using your school library or the internet, research the question, "Should you give to charity?" One perspective is that the world is unfair—the three wealthiest people in the world have more money than the 48 poorest countries combined, and millions of children die each year from poverty-related illnesses. So those who have more than they need should help those who lack enough resources to meet even basic needs. On the other hand, people deserve the money they have earned and should be able to spend it as they wish. Some people feel that charity demeans people and makes them dependent on others. Present your conclusion in a two-page report, providing examples from your research that support your answer.

 ## Words to Understand in This Chapter

anand karaj—Sikh marriage ceremony in the presence of the Guru Granth Sahib.

mantra—a syllable, word or phrase that is repeated while concentrating on it, leading, it is believed, to a higher level of spiritual experience.

ragi—musicians who accompany the singing of kirtan.

Vahiguru—often translated as "wonderful Lord"; one of the names used for God, often used as a mantra and sometimes referred to as the *gurmantra* ("God's mantra").

A Sikh groom leads his bride around the Guru Granth Sahib during the wedding ritual known as lavan, *or "circling."*

4 Family Matters and Ceremonies

S ikhs believe in one God and one humanity. The Guru Granth Sahib teaches that women and men are equal in both religious and worldly matters.

Guru Nanak said that both women and men could achieve union with God. The love that a woman has for her husband, he said, is an example of the love of a Sikh for God. He emphasized the importance of women in giving birth to, and caring for, rulers and kings. He also denied a belief held in Hindu and Muslim cultures that giving birth made a woman ritually polluted for a certain number of days.

Guru Amar Das appointed women as religious teachers. When Guru Gobind Singh founded the Khalsa, he asked his wife to place sugar crystals in the amrit water. To Hindus of the time, asking a woman to do this would be seen as making the amrit religiously polluted. But Sikhs did not believe this. Both women and men were eligible to become members of the Khalsa, and both had to obey the same rules.

Any role, or post of responsibility, in the Sikh community may be held by a woman or a man. In India in 1999, a woman, Bibi Jagjir Kaur, was elected president of the Shiromani Gurdwara Prabandhak Committee, the organization with legal responsibility for the care and management of all gurdwaras in the Punjab. In the United Kingdom, women have been elected members of gurdwara management committees, and in some cases have also been chosen as president.

In practice, however, most positions on the management committees are held by men. Women are often responsible for women's meetings or education, but are not usually given more public leadership positions, such as president or general secretary. Even though both women and men may read from the Guru Granth Sahib, there are fewer women serving as full-time granthi than men. Women are often found doing the more domestic tasks in the gurdwara while men occupy the more prominent roles. It has been argued that this is a reflection of the male-dominated culture found in the Punjab and, to a lesser extent, in the western nations like the United States, Canada, and the United Kingdom today. But it is not what the Guru Granth Sahib teaches.

Marriage in Sikh Culture

Marriage is very important in Sikhism. Guru Nanak taught that family life was the ideal kind of life. For a Sikh to

Musicians, known as ragis, chant and perform traditional music in the gurudwara during a Sikh wedding ceremony.

remain single throughout his or her life is unusual. In the Guru Granth Sahib, marriage is seen as the joining together of the *jot* in the two people. The sacred scripture says, "They are not man and wife who have only physical contact. Only those are truly married who have one spirit in two bodies."

The Rahit Maryada includes the statement that a Sikh should marry another Sikh. Apart from this, the choice of marriage partner lies with the couple themselves, and their decision will be respected by their parents. Traditionally

Wedding guests dance at a banquet in the Punjab.

parents suggest, but do not insist on, a particular partner, in what is known as an "assisted marriage."

The *anand karaj*, or wedding ceremony, takes place in the presence of the Guru Granth Sahib. It is the Guru Granth Sahib that is the witness to the marriage, not the people attending the ceremony. The bride and bridegroom show their agreement to their union by bowing before the sacred scripture. The prayer *Ardas* is recited, and the bride's father places garlands of flowers around the Guru Granth Sahib and around the necks of the bride and groom.

After this, a procedure called *lavan* ("circling") takes place. The bride's father gives one end of the bride's *chunni* (scarf) to the groom, who leads the bride in walking around the Guru Granth Sahib while first the musicians and then the congregation sing the four verses of the marriage hymn from the Guru Granth Sahib. The Ardas is repeated, and other prayers are recited. The Guru Granth Sahib is then opened at random to find verses that will give God's guidance to the couple, and *karah parshad* is distributed to the congregation. Sometimes, the bride and groom join the musicians and perform *kirtan*, to praise God at the start of their married life.

Educational Video

Scan here to view a highlights from a Sikh wedding.

Most Sikhs accept that sometimes marriages do break down. When this happens, both families will support the couple as best they can and try to help them overcome any difficulties. If it is obvious that the marriage is beyond repair, the couple may divorce. Divorcees are allowed to marry again.

Birth Control

Sikhs believe in maintaining the body's natural form, so they will not undergo surgery as a method of birth control. For example, vasectomies or the removal of the womb or ovaries, are forbidden unless they are for health reasons. Sikh teachings do not prohibit other forms of birth control, such as condoms or pills. However, contraception is

Shortly after a baby is born, the family consults the Guru Granth Sahib for guidance in choosing the first name. There is no difference between boys' and girls' names. The religious names Singh (for a boy) or Kaur (for a girl) will be added.

allowed only within marriage. Sex is regarded as an expression of love between a husband and wife, and not as wholly or mainly to have children.

Living together as husband and wife, but without formally marrying, is not acceptable. For young people to have sexual relations before marriage is completely against Sikh teaching. Even young people dating members of the opposite sex is not allowed, unless they go out with a group of friends, which would usually be acceptable. But if they were going to a disco or a party on their own, parents would be concerned.

There is no Sikh teaching specifically on abortion, but Sikhs are taught to respect all life. They believe that life begins at fertilization and is sacred. Abortion is therefore morally wrong. But although Sikhs find abortion unacceptable, even if the child may be born physically or mentally disabled, they also recognize the right of parents to make their own decisions. If the pregnancy is the result of rape, some Sikhs consider that an abortion may be justified.

Sikhs have always been opposed to the use of amniocentesis (examination of the embryo) to establish the gender of the unborn child. In some cultures, a son is seen to be of greater importance than a daughter, and if the fetus is female the family may want an abortion. Such a practice is illegal in India, and Sikhs regard it as infanticide. The Rahit Maryada says that Sikhs should not associate with anyone

Between Two Cultures

The film *Bend it like Beckham* (2001) shows how young Sikhs whose families had come to the United Kingdom in the 1960s live between two cultures: British society and their Sikh faith. The film tells the story of a Sikh girl who loves soccer. At first her family prohibits her from playing, but later she receives their support in realizing her dream.

who practices infanticide. In any case, Sikhs believe that both males and females are of equal worth.

Sikh Children

When a baby is only a few days old, the parents will go to the gurdwara to refer to the Guru Granth Sahib for guidance in the choice of name. There, the granthi prepares amrit, a mixture of water and sugar crystals, stirring the solution with a khanda (short, double-edged sword). At the same time, the granthi recites the first five verses of the morning prayer. He then wets the tip of a kirpan in the amrit he has prepared and touches the baby's tongue with it. The baby's mother drinks the rest of the amrit.

A name is chosen by opening the Guru Granth Sahib at random, reading aloud the passage at the top of the left-hand page, and selecting a name beginning with the first letter of the first word. The Sikh names Kaur (meaning "princess") for a girl or Singh (meaning "lion") for a boy are then added to the chosen name.

Sometimes a family that wishes to thank God for the gift of a new baby will arrange for an Akhand Path—a continuous reading of the Guru Granth Sahib from beginning to end. This takes 48 hours in total, each reader reading for two hours at a stretch. At the point of changeover, both readers will read a few lines together so there is no break in the reading. If family members can read the script of the Guru Granth Sahib, they are expected to take a turn reading. Otherwise, they listen to the readings. An Akhand Path reading may also be held to ask God's blessing for a forthcoming special event, such as a wedding, or moving house.

Funeral Rites

When a Sikh dies, the community participates in funeral rites. Before the funeral, the person's body is washed, clothed with the Five Ks, and placed in a coffin. Sometimes the coffin is taken to the gurdwara to allow friends and relatives to pay their last respects. While the coffin is being carried, people in the funeral procession recite the *mantras* "*Vahiguru*" and "Satnam Vahiguru." Often, the body is cremated and the ashes are scattered in flowing water.

 Text-Dependent Questions

1. What is an assisted marriage?
2. What is an Akhand Path?

 Research Project

Using the Internet or your school library, do some research to answer the question, "Can belief in reincarnation make people behave better?" Those who agree with such a statement may claim that if people believe they may be punished in their next life for their bad behavior in this one, they may think carefully before behaving badly, believing that the quickest and easiest way out of the cycle of reincarnation is to obey God. Those who disagree will probably contend that humans will always be selfish to some extent. They'll also note that most people only worry about the present, not about what might happen to them in years to come, or in their next lifetime. Present your conclusion in a two-page report, providing examples from your research that support your answer.

 Words to Understand in This Chapter

bhagat bani—the writings of Hindu and Muslim holy men that have been included in the Guru Granth Sahib.

kirat karo—to work honestly and give a proportion of what you earn to the poor; one of the responsibilities of all Sikhs.

Although many Sikhs are willing to use modern conveniences and technology, most also refuse to compromise the basic tenets of their faith in their daily lives.

5 Sikhism and the Modern World

In Sikhism, there is no idea of renouncing the world and living life as an ascetic, or of begging. The Guru Granth Sahib says, "He alone has found the right way who eats what he earns through toil and shares his earnings with the needy." The gurus taught that Sikhs should earn their living honestly, and be kind and generous to others.

In one story that is well known to Sikhs, Guru Nanak once chose to eat at the home of a humble carpenter, Bhai Lalo, rather than dining with Malik Bhago, the local Muslim leader. Malik Bhago was upset, so he asked the guru why he chose to eat with the workman instead of in the palace. Guru Nanak explained that Bhai Lalo earned his living honestly, whereas Malik Bhago made his money by exploiting the poor.

In 2004, Manmohan Singh became the first Sikh to be elected prime minister of India. He served in that position until 2014.

During his lifetime, Guru Nanak established a Sikh community at Kartarpur that lived according to his teachings. Although he was the leader, Nanak set an example to his community by doing manual labor in the afternoon.

Guru Nanak also taught that, "Truth is high, but higher still is truthful living." There are therefore some jobs that a Sikh should not do. According to the Rahit Maryada, a Sikh should not indulge in gambling or use alcohol, tobacco, or drugs, so any employment in industries involving these things—such as casinos or bars—should be avoided.

While some Sikhs do own or work in shops that sell tobacco or alcohol, typically Sikhs who have taken amrit would not do those jobs.

Unemployment is not an excuse for not working hard. Sikhs that lose their job can do *seva* in the gurdwara or other voluntary work until they can find other employment. Sikhs follow a principal called *kirat karo*, which requires them to work honestly and to give a proportion of what they earn back to the Sikh community, in order to help those who are less fortunate.

Respect for Other Religions

Sikhs believe that God can be found in all religions. Guru Gobind Singh said, "Hindus and Muslims are one. The same Being is creator and nourisher of all. Recognize no distinction between them." The sacred Sikh scripture, the Guru Granth Sahib, includes the *bhagat bani,* which are words of Hindu and Muslim holy men.

From the time of the gurus, Sikhism has taught respect for the right of people to worship God according to their own faith. When Guru Nanak said, "There is neither Hindu nor Muslim, therefore whose path shall I follow? I shall follow God's path," he was not criticizing Hinduism or Islam, but people who perform religious actions without ever thinking in any way about God. Guru Nanak believed that what was important was a person's individual relationship with God.

On many occasions, the gurus defended people of other religions. For example, Guru Amar Das persuaded the

Mughul government to remove a tax on Hindu pilgrims visiting the holy city of Hardwar. Guru Hargobind obtained the release of Hindu princes who had been unjustly imprisoned, before he would accept his own freedom. Guru Tegh Bahadur was respected by the Hindu Brahmins from Kashmir as a religious leader who was prepared to defend their own freedom of worship. The assistance that the guru provided for these Hindus. against the Muslim Mughal Emperor Aurangzeb of northern India, led to Tegh Bahadur's martyrdom.

Educational Video

To hear a sample of traditional Sikh music, scan here.

Sikhs tend to welcome members of other faiths. When the Mughul Emperor Akbar visited Guru Amar Das, he was told to eat langar, before meeting the Guru. The Harmandir Sahib in Amritsar was designed with four main entrances, emphasizing that anyone may enter. The foundation stone for the building was laid by Mian Mir, a local Muslim leader, at the invitation of Guru Arjan.

Anyone can attend a gurdwara, and people of different faiths may be invited to address the congregation on matters of general interest. Sikh voluntary service is also available to anyone who needs it, not just Sikhs. The *kirpan* worn by Sikhs reminds them of their duty to uphold the rights of all people, whatever their faith or beliefs.

Sikhs and the Natural World

The Mul Mantra says that God both created the world and is present in all creation. The Guru Granth Sahib states, "I see the Creator pervading everywhere." The sacred scripture also teaches that the world comes into being through God's will. The present tense is used, as Sikhs believe that

A Sikh musician perfoms a traditional raga *on an instrument called a* sarangi. *The sound of the* sarangi *is said to closely resemble the human voice.*

Members of a Sikh community march in a parade in Los Angeles.

creation is a continuous process that is ongoing. Thus, people have a responsibility to care for other living beings and to treat the environment with respect.

Puran Singh, who founded Pingalwala, a home for the sick and disabled, in Amritsar, typifies this caring attitude. As early as the 1960s, he protested against government policies, such as deforestation, that harmed the environment and deprived local villagers of the fuel they needed for cooking. To remain free to attack such policies, Puran Singh refused government support for his humanitarian work.

Today, the wealth of the Indian state of Punjab is based on agriculture, as Sikhs, like others, have made full use of modern technological developments. The use of high-yielding crops has brought economic prosperity, but created environmental problems. The Punjab is a land with five rivers, and a system of irrigation canals that carry the water to the fields. Now, the water level has fallen so much that the bore wells supplying fresh water to the villages need to be dug much deeper. Also, the use of artificial fertilizers has harmed the soil and threatens to pollute the rivers. To make matters worse, the use of genetically modified seeds has made farmers more dependent on fertilizers and ruined some of them financially.

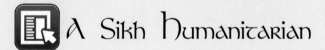 A Sikh Humanitarian

Puran Singh was born in 1904 to a Hindu family in India. However, as a young man he converted to Sikhism and dedicated his life to *seva*. In 1934, while living in Lahore (now part of Pakistan), he found an abandoned baby who was disabled. From then on, he cared for the child, whom he called Piara Singh, carrying him on his back as he went around helping others. In 1947, when British India was divided into the countries of India and Pakistan, he cared for refugees. Puran Singh later founded Pingalwala, meaning "home for the disabled," which cares for people who are sick, disabled or dying. In 1991 Puran Singh was nominated for the Nobel Peace Prize. He died in 1992, but his work continues.

Sikhs and Modern Medicine

From the time of the Gurus, Sikhs have been involved in caring for the sick. Guru Nanak is said to have healed people suffering from leprosy, an infectious disease that in the fifteenth century was incurable. Guru Arjan founded a hospital to care for lepers.

In the modern world, it is acceptable for Sikhs to donate their organs after death for use in transplant surgery. This is because of the Sikh belief that, when someone dies, that person's *jot* leaves the body and has no more use for it. The

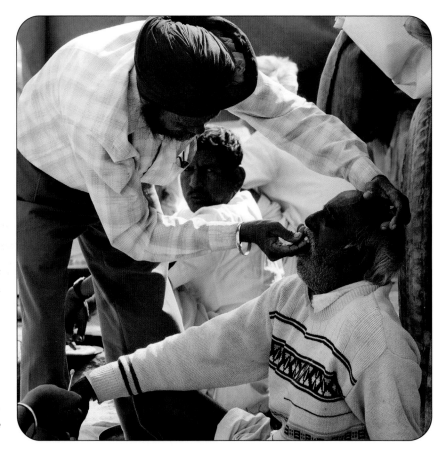

A Sikh dentist examines a man's teeth in Rajasthan, India.

Guru Granth Sahib says, "The dead may be cremated or buried, or thrown to the dogs, or cast into the waters, or down an empty well. No one knows where the soul goes and disappears to." In 1987 a Sikh established the "Life After Death Society" in Calcutta to encourage people to donate their bodies for transplant surgery and medical research after their death.

In India, blindness due to damage to the cornea is a serious problem. The Guru Ram Das Mission in the U.K. financially supports hospitals and eye clinics in the Punjab. Eye clinics in India have also been sponsored for several years by a west London gurdwara in Hounslow. The gurdwara has also organized meetings to encourage its members to donate bone marrow.

Not all medical practices are acceptable to Sikhs. Artificial insemination, for example, is permitted only if the husband's sperm and wife's egg are used. The use of donor eggs or sperm is regarded as no better than adultery.

Many Sikhs would consider that altering the structure of human cells, even if it is done to prevent the spread of a genetic illness, is wrong. If life begins at fertilization, then genetic engineering is altering the living form that God has given. Some Sikhs, however, disagree and believe that such medical knowledge is God-given and should be used to help people.

Sikh Views on War and Violence

Sikhs have a centuries-old reputation as brave warriors. According to the teachings of the Gurus, Sikhs have a responsibility not only for the spiritual, but also for the temporal—what takes place in the world. But it was not until Guru Hargobind became Guru in 1606, after the martyrdom of Guru Arjan, that Sikhs formed a standing army. This army was not for starting a war, but for protecting Sikhs who were being persecuted. When the Hindu Brahmins asked for Guru Tegh Bahadur's protection, the Guru went to see the Mughul emperor to intercede for them, but he did not take an army with him.

Guru Gobind Singh led his army in many battles against the Mughuls, but only because Sikhs were being attacked. Guru Gobind Singh further introduced *dharam yudh*—the just war theory—to limit the scale of death and injury. In one battle, a Sikh, Bhai Khanaiya, was seen tending wounded soldiers in both the Sikh and the Mughul armies. He was brought before Guru Gobind Singh to explain his actions. But the Guru praised Bhai Khanaiya for caring for all the injured, not just those on his own side.

Guru Gobind Singh emphasized that any war fought by Sikhs must be a just one. "I have no ambition but to wage righteous war," he said. The *kirpan* that Sikhs wear is a reminder of God's care for them, and of their duty to care for those that are discriminated against or treated unfairly.

Unfortunately, Since the September 11 terrorist attacks, there has been an increase of violence against Sikh Americans. In the days after the terrorist attacks, some Americans confused Sikhs for Muslims because of their turbans and distinctively different appearance. Sikhs reported being harassed and injured. Some were even

Sikh "Just War" Theory

A "just war" is a conflict that is considered to be justifiable or legitimate for moral or religious regions. Most people, for example, would not consider Iraq's invasion of Kuwait in 1990 to be justified, as that conflict was initiated for the illegal transfer of land and resources from one country (Kuwait) to another (Iraq). However, the international coalition, led by the United States, that drove Iraqi forces out of Kuwait could be considered a "just war" because it was fought to achieve the limited aim of reversing Iraq's aggression.

Guru Gobind Singh established a set of principles that would determine whether a conflict is a "just war." These principals, known as *dharam yudh*, include the following:

- War should be used only as a last resort, when all other efforts to find peace have failed.
- No war should be started out of anger or for revenge.
- Any property taken during a war must be returned afterward, looting is strictly forbidden, and no territory captured should be kept after the war.
- The army should be made up of only paid soldiers, who must obey the Sikh code of conduct.
- Women should at all times be treated with respect.
- Only the minimum amount of force needed should be used, and the war should be stopped once its aim is achieved.

killed. Four days after the terrorist attacks, Balbir Singh Sodhi, a Sikh working at a gas station in Arizona, was murdered by a man who wanted to kill Muslims in revenge.

The Sikh Coalition, an advocacy group, estimates that over 700 hate crimes have been committed against Sikhs since September 11, 2001. That number, averaged out, totals more than one attack a week for more than fifteen years. And some of these attacks are fatal, such as the 2011 murder of two elderly Sikh men wearing traditional dress in California, or a 2012 assault in Wisconsin in which a

Sikhs in Auckland, New Zealand, protest against the violence and discrimination that Sikhs in other countries sometimes experience.

member of a white-supremacist group killed six Sikhs and wounded four other people in a shooting at a gurdwara.

As a result, some American Sikhs have opted to change their appearance to better fit in to western society. They cut their hair and stop wearing the traditional turban and clothing. Others, however, refuse to compromise their religious beliefs. The Sikh Coalition and other Sikh activist groups give presentations on Sikhism to everyone from kindergarteners to police officers to airport workers, hoping to create a greater understanding of their religion.

 Text-Dependent Questions

1. Why did Guru Nanak choose to eat a meal with a humble carpenter, rather than a Muslim ruler?
2. What is the *bhagat bani*?
3. What guru developed the theory known as *dharam yudh*?

 Research Project

Using the Internet or your school library, do some research to answer the question, "Is violence ever justified? On one hand, some people argue that the principle of "an eye for an eye" would leave the whole world blind. If people are strong enough, they contend, they can overcome evil with love. Others believe that while violence is wrong, it may also be the lesser of two evils—for example, it is good to overthrow a dictator whose actions cause innocent people to suffer. Present your conclusion in a two-page report, providing examples from your research that support your answer.

Religious Demographics

U.S. & Canada about 5.6 million people

Europe about 2.1 million people

Europe about 0.5 million people

Europe about 550 million people

Canada about 25 million people

Asia about 550 million people

U.S. about 225 million people

U.S. about 0.575 million

Europe about 50 million people

Asia about 1179 million people

Asia about 350 million people

Israel about 5.6 million people

North and South America about 10 million people

Africa about 518 million people

India about 18 million people

Asia about 950 million people

Latin America about 543 million people

Africa about 475 million people

Australia and Oceania about 24 million people

Australia and Oceania about 0.7 million people

Christians
about 2.2 billion people

Muslims
about 1.6 billion people

Sikh
about 23 million people

Hindus
about 1 billion people

Jews
about 14 million people

Buddhist
about 576 million people

Christian 31.5%	Islam 22.3%	No religion 15.4%	Hindu 14.0%	Buddhist 5.3%	Sikhism 0.3%	Judaism 0.2%	Others 11%

Hinduism

Founded
Developed gradually in prehistoric times

Number of followers
Around 1 billion

Holy Places
River Ganges, especially at Varanasi (Benares). Several other places in India

Holy Books
Vedas, Upanishads, Mahabharata, Rarnayana

Holy Symbol
Aum

Buddhism

Founded
535 BCE in Northern India

Number of followers
Around 576 million

Holy Places
Bodh Gaya, Sarnath, both in northern India

Holy Books
Tripitaka

Holy Symbol
Eight-spoked wheel

Sikhism

Founded
Northwest India, 15th century CE

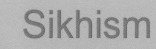

Number of followers
Around 23 million

Holy Places
There are five important, takhts, or seats of high authority: in Amritsar, Patna Sahib, Anandpur Sahib, Nanded, and Talwandi

Holy Books
The Guru Granth Sahib

Holy Symbol
The Khanda, the symbol of the Khalsa

Christianity

Founded
Around 30 CE, Jerusalem

Number of followers
Around 2.2 billion

Holy Places
Jerusalem and other sites
associated with the life of Jesus

Holy Books
The Bible
(Old and New Testament)

Holy Symbol
Cross

Judaism

Founded
In what is now Israel, around 2,000 BCE

Number of followers
Around 14 million

Holy Places
Jerusalem, especially
the Western Wall

Holy Books
The Torah

Holy Symbol
Seven-branched menorah (candle stand)

Islam

Founded
610 CE on the Arabian Peninsula

Number of followers
Around 1.6 billion

Holy Places
Makkah and Madinah, in Saudi Arabia

Holy Books
The Qur'an

Holy Symbol
Crescent and star

Quick Reference: Sikhism

Worldwide distribution

There are roughly 23 million Sikhs in the world, making Sikhism the world's fifth-largest religion.

More than 93 percent of all Sikhs live in and around the Indian subcontinent. Some 20.7 million Sikhs (90 percent of the total population) live in India. Significant Sikh communities can also be found in Bangladesh (100,000 Sikhs) and Pakistan (20,000 Sikhs). Countries of southeast Asia are also home to Sikh communities, including Malaysia (100,000 Sikhs) and Thailand (70,000 Sikhs). Australia is home to about 72,000 Sikhs.

The largest group of Sikhs to be found outside of south or southeast Asia lives in North America. Canada is home to the second-largest Sikh community, at more than 600,000 people (about 2 percent of the total Sikh population). The United States is home to the fourth-largest Sikh community at roughly 250,000 people.

In Europe, the United Kingdom is home to the largest Sikh population, at roughly 430,000 people. This is due to the long historical association of India as part of the British Empire. Elsewhere in Europe, Italy (70,000 Sikhs), Germany (35,000 Sikhs), and Greece (20,000 Sikhs) have sizeable communities, while there are more modestly sized Sikh communities in such countries as Belgium, France, and the Netherlands.

Sikhs have also immigrated to Africa, with about 100,000 living in the east African nations of Kenya, Tanzania, and Uganda. About 35,000 Sikhs live in the small island nation of Mauritius; they make up 3 percent of the country's population.

Calendar and Major Festivals

The dates given below are according to the Nanakshahi calendar, which was approved in 2003 by the Shiromani Gurdwara Parbandhak Committee in Amritsar. In the Nanakashahi calendar, the Sikh year begins with Vaisakhi, which falls on April 14. It commemorates the institution of the Khalsa by Guru Gobind Singh in 1699.

Other notable dates in the Nanakshahi calendar include June 16 (commemorating the martyrdom of Guru Arjan); August 16 (installation of the Adi Granth, the first authorized collection of gurbani); October 20 (the date that the Guru Granth Sahib was said to end the line of human Gurus) and October 21 (the martyrdom of Guru Gobind Singh); and November 24 (the martyrdom of Guru Tegh Bahadur, who died upholding the religious freedom of Hindus and Sikhs).

On November 8, Sikhs observe the birthday of Guru Nanak. Although Nanak was actually born on April 14, the occasion is celebrated on this date to avoid two important Sikh events being celebrated on the same day. The birthdate of Guru Gobind Singh is celebrated on January 5.

A Sikh woman gives away rice on the streets of Delhi, India, during the Guru Nanak Gurpurab observation. This festival celebrates the birth of the first Sikh Guru.

Sikhism Timeline

1469	Birth of Guru Nanak.
1499	Guru Nanak taken into God's presence and given his life's work of meditating on God's name, and teaching others to do the same.
1538–39	Death of Guru Nanak, who was succeeded by Lahina, known as Guru Angad.
1552	Death of Guru Angad and succession of Guru Amar Das.
1574	Death of Guru Amar Das and succession of Guru Ram Das.
1581	Death of Guru Ram Das and succession of Guru Arjan.
1603–04	Compilation of the Adi Granth under the supervision of Guru Arjan.
1604	Completion of the Harmandir Sahib (Golden Temple) in Amritsar, and installation of the Adi Granth by Guru Arjan.
1606	Martyrdom of Guru Arjan and succession of Guru Hargobind.
1644	Death of Guru Hargobind and succession of Guru Har Rai.
1661	Death of Guru Har Rai and succession of Guru

Har Krishnan.

1664	Death of Guru Har Krishnan and succession of Guru Tegh Bahadur.
1675	Martyrdom of Guru Tegh Bahadur and succession of Guru Gobind Singh.
1699	Introduction of the institution of the Khalsa by Guru Gobind Singh at Anandpur Sahib on the festival of Vaisakhi.
1708	Death of Guru Gobind Singh and succession of the Guru Granth Sahib, ending the line of human Gurus.
1801	Ranjit Singh becomes sovereign, or Maharajah, of the Sikh state of Punjab and supervises the gold plating and marble facing of the Harmandir Sahib.
1909	Anand Marriage Act passed, stating that the Anand Karaj is the only approved order for Sikh marriages.
1919	Jallianwala Bagh Massacre in Amritsar, near the Harmandir Sahib. Some 1200 Sikhs killed, and many more injured, when British army troops fired on a peaceful crowd of Sikhs gathered there.
1925	Sikh Gurdwaras Act passed in India, giving the Sikh community responsibility for managing gurdwaras in the Punjab. The Shiromani Gurdwara Parbandhak Committee, established in 1920, is chosen by the Sikhs to have this responsibility.

1947	Partition of the Punjab, following Indian independence from the U.K., resulting in mass migration of Hindus and Sikhs from Pakistan, and of Muslims from Indian Punjab. Many Sikh sacred places, including Guru Nanak's birthplace of Talwandi, now in Pakistan Punjab.
1984	The Indian army, acting on the orders of prime minister Indira Gandhi, attack the Harmandir Sahib complex on 4 June. Jarnail Singh Bhindranwale, the leading campaigner for an independent Sikh state, is among those killed in the attack. On 31 October Indira Gandhi is assassinated, allegedly by one of her Sikh bodyguards, leading to a massacre of Sikhs, particularly in Delhi and New Delhi.
1985	Indian prime minister Rajiv Gandhi signs a Memorandum of Settlement awarding, among other things, Chandigarh to Punjab. Sikh leader Harchand Singh Longowal is assassinated while speaking at a gurdwara on August 20.
1986	On January 26, an independent Sikh state called Khalistan is proclaimed during a large gathering of Sikhs at Amritsar.
1990	Harminder Singh Sandhu, president of the All India Sikh Students Federation (A.I.S.S.F.), is assassinated.

1998   Ranjit Singh, head priest of the Akal Takht in Amritsar, issues an edict declaring that participants in *langar* could not sit on benches and chairs during the communal meal. The Nanakshahi calendar begins to be implemented, although it will take many years before a majority of Sikhs accept the new calendar.

1999   Sikhs celebrate the tercentenary (300 year anniversary) of the birth of the Khalsa.

2004   Manmohan Singh becomes the first Sikh elected as prime minister of India. He serves two terms in the post, leaving office in 2014.

Series Glossary of Key Terms

afterlife—a term that refers to a continuation of existence beyond the natural world, or after death.

BCE and CE—alternatives to the traditional Western designation of calendar eras, which used the birth of Jesus as a dividing line. BCE stands for "Before the Common Era," and is equivalent to BC ("Before Christ"). Dates labeled CE, or "Common Era," are equivalent to *Anno Domini* (AD, or "the Year of Our Lord").

chant—the rhythmic speaking or singing of words or sounds, intended to convey emotion in worship or to express the chanter's spiritual side. Chants can be conducted either on a single pitch or with a simple melody involving a limited set of notes, and often include a great deal of repetition.

creation—the beginnings of humanity, earth, life, and the universe. According to most religions, creation was a deliberate act by a supreme being.

deity (or god)—a supernatural being, usually considered to have significant power. Deities/gods are worshipped and considered sacred by human beings. Some deities are believed to control time and fate, to be the ultimate judges of human worth and behavior, and to be the designers and creators of the Earth or the universe. Others are believed to control natural phenomena, such as lightning, floods, and storms. They can assume a variety of forms, but are frequently depicted as having human or animal form, as well as specific personalities and characteristics.

hymn—a song specifically written as a song of praise, adoration or prayer, typically addressed to a god or deity.

miracle—according to many religions, a miracle is an unusual example of divine intervention in the universe by a god or deity, often one in which natural laws are overruled, suspended, or modified.

prayer—an effort to communicate with a deity or god, or another form of spiritual entity. Prayers are usually intended to offer praise, to make a request, or simply to express the person's thoughts and emotions.

prophecy—the prediction of future events, thanks to either direct or indirect communication with a deity or god. The term prophecy is also used to describe the revelation of divine will.

Sikhs participate in a ceremony at Gurudwara Bangla Sahib, one of the most prominent Sikh temples in India.

A Sikh performs evening prayers while seated in the lotus position.

religion—a system of belief concerning the supernatural, sacred, or divine; and the moral codes, practices, values, institutions and rituals associated with such belief. There are many different religions in the world today.

ritual—a formal, predetermined set of symbolic actions generally performed in a particular environment at a regular, recurring interval. The actions that make up a ritual often include, but are not limited to, such things as recitation, singing, group processions, repetitive dance, and manipulation of sacred objects. The general purpose of rituals is to engage a group of people in unified worship, in order to strengthen their communal bonds.

saint—a term that refers to someone who is considered to be exceptionally virtuous and holy. It can be applied to both the living and the dead and is an acceptable term in most of the world's popular religions. A saint is held up as an example of how all other members of the religious community should act.

worship—refers to specific acts of religious praise, honor, or devotion, typically directed to a supernatural being such as a deity or god. Typical acts of worship include prayer, sacrifice, rituals, meditation, holidays and festivals, pilgrimages, hymns or psalms, the construction of temples or shrines, and the creation of idols that represent the deity.

Organizations to Contact

American Sikh Council (ASC)
P.O. Box 932
Voorhees, NJ 08043
Phone: 607-269-7454
Email:
contact@americansikhcouncil.org
Website: http://www.american-
sikhcouncil.org

Association of Sikh Professionals
PO Box 140
Hopewell, VA 23860
Phone: 804-541-9290
Website: www.sikhprofessionals.org

**Council of Khalistan,
International Sikh Organization**
730 24th Street NW, Suite 310
Washington, DC 20037
Phone: 202-337-1904
Website: www.khalistan.com

Sikh Center
13515 Wimbledon Oaks Dr.
Houston, TX 77065
Phone: 281-955-2340
Website: http://sikhcenterhouston.org

Sikh Coalition
PO Box 7132
New York, NY 10150-7132
Website: www.sikhcoalition.org

**Sikh Council on Research and
Education**
3123-1 University Blvd., W.
Kensington, MD 20895
Phone: 301-949-8439
Website: www.sikhcouncilusa.org

The Sikh Cultural Society
95-30 118th Street
Richmond Hill, NY 11419
Phone: 718-846-9144
Website:
   www.sikh.net/Gurdwara/SCSNY

Sikh Cultural Society of W. New
York / Buffalo Gurdwara Sahib
6569 Main Street
Williamsville, NY 14221
Phone: 716-632-3849
Website: www.members.aol.com/
   BuffaloGurdwara

Sikh Educational and Religious
Foundation
P.O. Box 1553
Dublin, OH 43017
Phone: 614-210-0591
Website: http://www.serf.ws

Sikh Youth Federation
6863 Cloister Road
Toledo, OH 43617
Phone: 419-841-7178

The Sikh Foundation, USA
580 College Avenue
Palo Alto, CA 94306
Phone: 650-494-7454
Website: www.sikhfoundation.org

Sikh Heritage Institute
5 Hillock Ct.
Huntington, NY 11743
Phone: 631-754-8718

Sikh Mediawatch and Resource
Task Force
1331 H Street, NW, 11th Floor
Washington, DC 20005
Phone: 202-393-2700
Website: www.sikhmediawatch.org

United Sikh Religious and
Educational Foundation
15302 Morris Bridge Road
Tampa, FL 33602
Phone: 813-986-6205

Sikh Youth Federation of North America
170 Longview Avenue
White Plains, NY 10605
Phone: 914-428-6950

World Sikh Council—America Region
P.O. Box 3635
Columbus, Ohio 43210, USA
Phone: 614-210-0591
Fax: 419-535-6794
Email:
   contact@worldsikhcouncil.org
Website: www.worldsikhcouncil.org

World Sikh Organization of Canada
1181 Cecil Avenue
Ottawa, ON K1H 7Z6
Canada
Phone: (613) 521-1984
Email: balpreetsingh@worldsikh.org
Website: www.worldsikh.ca

A Sikh pilgrim prays in a holy tank near the golden temple (Sri Harmandir Sahib) of Amritsar, India.

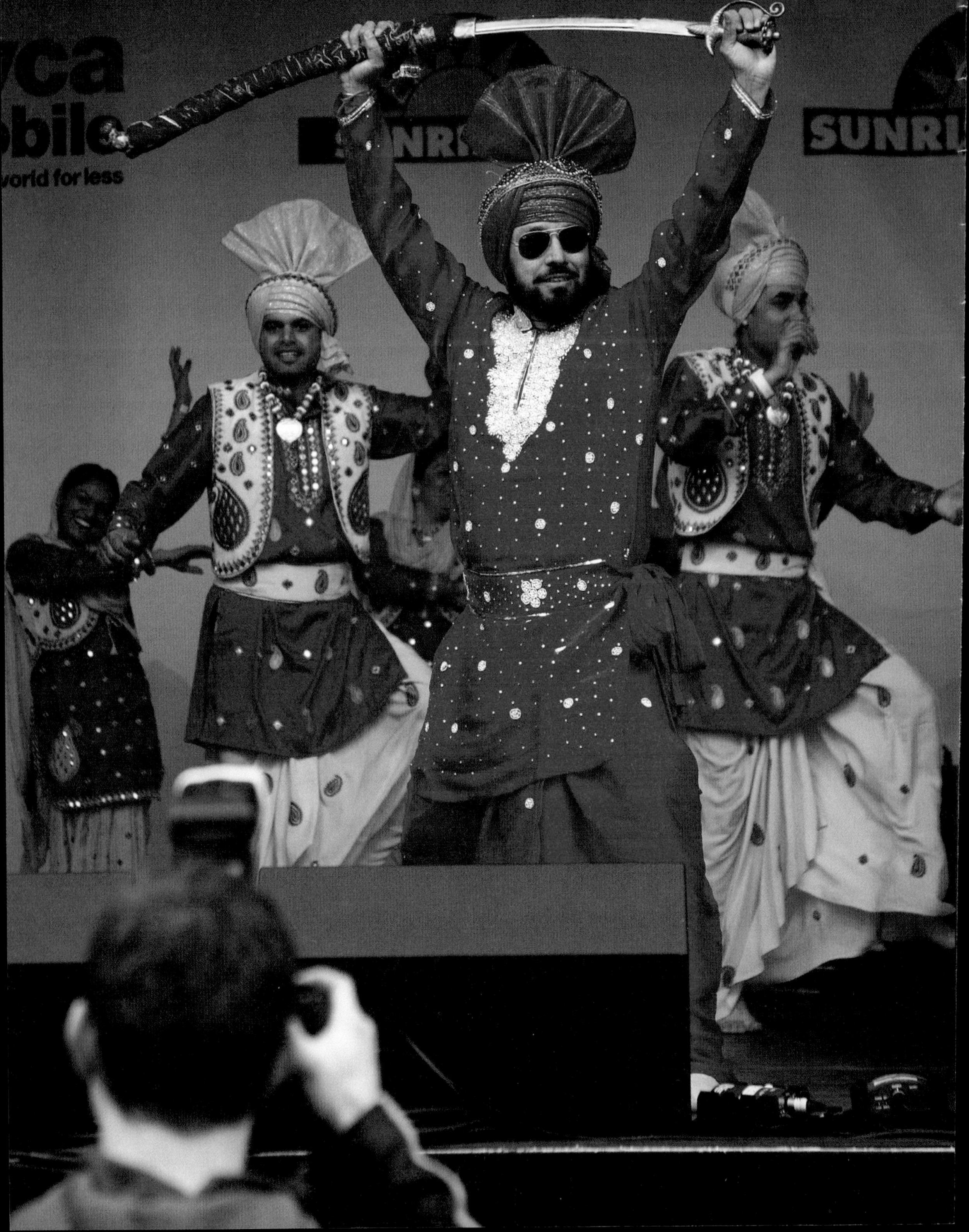
world for less
SUNRI

Further Reading

Bowker, John. *World Religions: The Great Faiths Explored and Explained*. London: Dorling Kindersley Ltd., 2006.

Jakobsh, Doris. *Sikhism*. Honolulu: University of Hawaii Press, 2012.

McDermott, Gerald R. *World Religions: An Indispensable Introduction*. Nashville, Tenn.: Thomas Nelson, 2011.

Mandair, Arvind-Pal Singh. *Sikhism: A Guide for the Perplexed*. New York: Bloomsbury Publishing PLC, 2013.

Prothero, Stephen. *God Is Not One: The Eight Rival Religions that Run the World*. New York: HarperCollins, 2010.

Shackle, Christopher, and Arvind Mandair, editors. *Teachings of the Sikh Gurus: Selections from the Sikh Scriptures*. 1st ed. New York: Routledge, 2005.

Singh, Nikky-Guninder Kaur. *Sikhism: An Introduction*. New York: I.B. Tauris & Co., 2011.

Smith, Huston. *The World's Religions*. New York: HarperCollins, 2009.

Internet Resources

www.sikhs.org

This website is a reference resource about Sikhism. It includes information about the belief system, development, history and practices of the Sikh religion, as well as a complete English transaltion of the Guru Granth Sahib, the Sikh scripture.

www.bbc.co.uk/religion/religions/sikhism/

This page from the British Broadcasting Company (BBC) provides information about Sikh beliefs, customs, history, and ethics.

www.pewresearch.org/topics/muslims-and-islam

This page run by the Pew Research Center provides links to polls and articles about the opinions and attitudes of people living in India, as well as articles on Sikhs and Indians in the United States and other countries.

www.cia.gov/library/publications/the-world-factbook

The CIA World Factbook is a convenient source of basic information about any country in the world. This site includes links to a page on each country with religious, geographic, demographic, economic, and governmental data.

http://aianational.com

The Association of Indians in America (AIA) is the oldest national association of Asian Indians in America. The organization concerns itself with the social welfare of South Asians who have decided to live in the United States.

www.sacred-texts.com

The Internet Sacred Text Archive has an enormous repository of electronic texts about religion, mythology, legends and folklore, and occult and esoteric topics.

www.indius.org

Indian Americans Involved in the U.S (IndiUS) is a forum created to share news and articles that promote the culture of Indian Americans and encourage community involvement.

www.iado.org

The homesite of the Indo-American Democratic Organization (IADO), a lobby group that serves Indian Americans and is engaged in issues concerning them, including immigration, education, and hate crimes.

Index

Numbers in **bold italics** refer to captions.

About the Author

Jennifer Burton received her BA in English-Creative Writing from Western Michigan University and her MA in English at the University of Florida, where she specialized in cultural studies. She has written biographies for various publications and is currently working on a book of poems and short stories with her husband. She teaches tenth grade English in Texas, where she lives with her husband and their Labrador retriever, Shadow.